LADYBUGOLOGY

LADYBUGOLOGY

by Michael Elsohn Ross

photographs by Brian Grogan • illustrations by Darren Erickson

Carolrhoda Books, Inc. / Minneapolis

To Davy Douglass and our bug adventures

Special thanks to Carl Brownless, Phyllis Weber, and their students at the El Portal Elementary School, California

Additional photographs courtesy of: © Robert and Linda Mitchell, pp. 27, 28, 30.

Text copyright © 1997 by Michael Elsohn Ross
Photographs copyright © 1997 by Brian Grogan
Illustrations copyright © 1997 by Carolrhoda Books, Inc.

Carolrhoda Books, Inc., c/o The Lerner Publishing Group
241 First Avenue North, Minneapolis, MN 55401 U.S.A.

LIBRARY OF CONGRESS CATALOGING-IN-PUBLICATIONS DATA

Ross, Michael Elsohn
    Ladybugology / by Michael Elsohn Ross ; photographs by Brian Grogan ; illustrations by Darren Erickson.
        p.   cm.
    Includes index.
    Summary: Describes the physical characteristics, habits, and life of ladybugs and provides instructions for finding, collecting, and keeping these beetles as pets.
    ISBN 1-57505-051-X
    1. Ladybugs—Juvenile literature. 2. Ladybugs—Experiments—Juvenile literature.
3. Ladybugs as pets—Juvenile literature. [1. Ladybugs. 2. Ladybugs as pets.] I. Grogan, Brian, ill. II. Erickson, Darren, ill. III. Title.
QL596.C65R67 1997
595.76'9—cd21   96-37441

Manufactured in the United States of America
1 2 3 4 5 6 – JR – 02 01 00 99 98 97

Contents

Run a leafy track.

Eat a sugary snack,

like a busy backyard ladybug

with dots all over its back.

You've probably met a ladybug before. Perhaps you know that ladybugs are often red with black dots and they like to crawl around on plants, but what else do you know? Have you ever really been introduced to a ladybug?

Welcome to Ladybug Land

Called ladybugs by most folks, these creatures are also known as ladybird beetles. Though they are neither ladies nor birds, they are beetles. Some people are frightened by all little critters like ladybugs, but you'll find that ladybugs don't sting or scratch. They may occasionally give you a nip, but it's nothing that requires a Band-Aid.

Biologists are scientists who study living things. Ornithologists are adventurers who study birds. Ladybugologists are backyard explorers who look into the lives of their ladybug neighbors. They are also scientists who handle small critters with gentleness and respect. You don't need to hurt anything to be a ladybugologist. In fact, the more careful you are with the little creatures, the more you will learn. All you need to do is open your eyes and watch the small bug dramas playing in your own backyard.

Most folks notice ladybugs because they are as bright and shiny as a fire engine. Ladybugs are easy to see—unless they are resting on a bright red tomato. But a ladybug on a green leaf is hard to miss. During fall and winter in some parts of the world, ladybugs can be found in large clumps in bark crevices, on boulders, or even in old houses or barns. In spring and summer, ladybugs can be seen flying through the air or crawling up and down plants.

To catch your local ladybugs, all you need is a plastic jar (with a lid) and sharp eyes. As you scan leaves, stems, and rocks, focus on any bits of red or orange that you see. Once you spot a

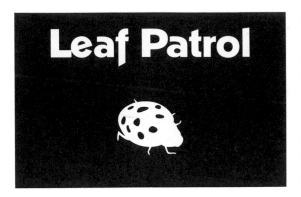

Leaf Patrol

ladybug, swiftly place the open jar beneath the leaf or stem and tap the ladybug into it. Quickly snap on the lid to prevent the ladybug from escaping. As you search for ladybugs, you may also notice small creatures that look like miniature alligators dressed for Halloween. These are young ladybugs, or ladybug **larvae** (LAHR-vee).

Though ladybugs are not hazardous to humans, think about how the people at your house might react to having ladybugs as temporary pets. If your family members are sometimes frightened by small crawling creatures, you may want to show them this article from the famous fictional newspaper *The Busy Bee.*

The Right Visitors

Matilda and Alfie Archer finally found a pet their folks agreed to keep in their modest mobile home in Zolfo Springs, Florida.

"Gators are too big, sharks are too wet, and I can't stand the smell of skunks," declared their dad. "Dogs bark too much, cats scratch too much, and camels spit," explained their mom. "Ladybugs don't eat much. They don't bark, scratch, or spit, and they only stink a teeny-weeny bit," explained Matilda and Alfie as they showed their folks the ladybugs they had discovered in their backyard. Though they were a bit put off by pesky mosquitoes and other bloodsucking bugs, Mr. and Mrs. Archer sighed with relief on seeing the little ladybugs. They were so quiet and cheerful looking that Mr. and Mrs. Archer just couldn't say no—and they didn't!

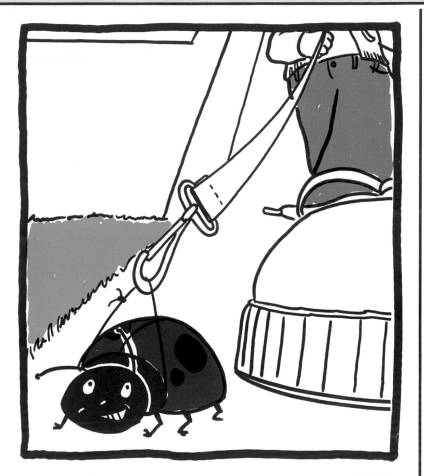

Ladybugs don't require a motel room, but they do need a place where they will be safe. Are you ready to have some ladybugs as guests? Just follow these simple instructions to create a luxurious ladybug lodge.

keep it in your room, back porch, or garage. But ladybugs, like most critters, can be harmed by too much heat. A jar left in direct sunlight gets pretty toasty. Cool temperatures can relax your guests, and cool ladybugs can go several days without food (for information on what ladybugs eat, see pages 28 and 30). And no matter how nice your ladybug lodge is, it will never be the same as a ladybug's real home. After your ladybugs have been visiting for a few days, be a good pal and return them to their backyard stomping grounds.

You will need:

✔ a clear plastic jar or food container
✔ fresh leaves
✔ plastic wrap or a plastic bag
✔ a rubber band
✔ a straight pin
✔ a piece of paper or cardboard

1. Place some leaves inside the container.
2. Invite some ladybugs for a visit.
3. Cover the opening with a piece of plastic wrap and secure it with a rubber band. Using a pin, poke some small airholes in the plastic.
4. With the paper or cardboard, make a sign announcing, "Ladybug Lodge," so nobody mistakes it for a plain old container of leaves.

This ladybug lodge will work fine, whether you

What if you were the pet of some ten-story-high giant? If your roof was clear, the giant could watch you eat, sleep, and play. For privacy, you could crawl under your bed or make a tent with blankets. Now imagine that you are the giant. This should be simple, since you really are a giant compared to a bug the size of one of your fingernails.

Nosy Giant

Peek through the roof of the ladybug lodge. What do you see? Keep a piece of paper next to the lodge and jot down every new thing you notice. Though the ladybugs may not be brushing their teeth or watching television, they are probably up to some unusual antics. Are they always doing the same thing, or is there some variety in their routine? Show your list of ladybug activities to some friends, and challenge them to catch sight of the ladybugs doing some different things. Who knows what you may all discover!

You have probably noticed by now that ladybugs are talented climbers. Perhaps they have become tired of the cramped quarters of your ladybug lodge and could use some real exercise in a professional climbing gym. You can construct a climbing gym for your friends in a large plastic dish tub.

Climbing Gym

You will need:

- ✔ a plastic dish tub or other container
- ✔ a small branch
- ✔ modeling clay
- ✔ string or yarn
- ✔ stones
- ✔ toy cars
- ✔ pencils
- ✔ balls or marbles
- ✔ anything else you think a ladybug can climb
- ✔ ladybugs

In your container, arrange some of the items listed to make a world-class climbing gym. Use modeling clay to make a stand for the branch, for some pencils, and for anything else you'd like to make stand up. Tie some string or yarn to your branch for rope ladders. Add any other climbing items to complete your gym. Place the climbing gym outside or in a place where it will be okay if your ladybugs decide to fly.

When your climbing gym is ready, add a ladybug. What does it climb? Can it climb everything? Add a few more ladybugs to the gym. What happens?

Now it's your turn to be a giant jungle gym. Place a ladybug on your arm and watch it. Can it climb over arm hairs? Does it tickle? Be sure to return the ladybugs to their lodge once exercise time is up. Your folks will probably rather have them in the safety of their ladybug home than flying down the hallways.

Are you aware? Would you notice if your best friend wore a wig or if your principal got a tattoo? Would you notice if your father shaved his legs? Do you pick up on small details? Whatever your answers, the Aware Dare is for you. If you are completely tuned out, this game will help you tune in to tiny details. Being tuned in is extremely helpful when you are becoming familiar with new friends, such as ladybugs. If you are sharp-eyed, this game will allow you to show off your keen talents. Though it can be played alone, the Aware Dare is more challenging with two or more players.

You will need:

✔ one ladybug
✔ a clear drinking glass or plastic container
✔ a magnifying lens
✔ optional: a pen or pencil and paper

How to Play:

1. Place the ladybug on a hard surface, and put the glass or container upside down over it.

2. Decide who is going to go first.

3. Beginning with player number one, take turns sharing ladybug observations. For example, someone might say, "It's red," or "It crawls." Any detail is okay, but no repeats are allowed. More items can be added to someone else's observation, however. For example, someone may have said, "It has dots," but another person can still say, "It has six dots."

Optional: Pick one player to write down what each of you notices.

4. Continue taking turns in the same order until only one player is able to make a new observation. The last person to share a ladybug characteristic is the most aware.

5. Return the ladybug to its lodge.

Math Bugs

Before computer math games even existed, there were ladybugs to depend on for mathematical entertainment. No doubt you have counted the dots on a ladybug's back. That's math. Or maybe you have watched a ladybug racing up a plant stem and tried to guess its speed. That's math. Ladybugs are math bugs, and you can get to know them better by trying some of these investigations.

You will need:

✔ a ladybug
✔ a watch or clock
✔ a sheet of paper
✔ a pen or pencil
✔ a measuring tape
✔ chalk
✔ a magnifying lens
✔ one cup of dried split peas

Speed: How fast does a ladybug move? Place one in the middle of a sheet of paper and see how long it takes to crawl off. To see how far a ladybug can go in a minute, let one loose on a large, flat surface, such as a sidewalk. Mark the starting point, then watch the ladybug for one minute. Mark the ending point, then measure the distance between the points. If your ladybug flies away, see if you can measure the distance it travels. How fast can you cover the same distance at a run, walk, or crawl?

Ladybug Lines: Do you always walk in a straight line? Does a ladybug? Place a ladybug on a paved surface and mark its trail with chalk. Try this with several ladybugs and use different colored chalk for each. Look at the chalk lines from above. What do you notice?

Paired Parts: Like people, ladybugs have parts that come in pairs. Make a list of ladybug parts. How many did you come up with? Are there any parts that aren't in pairs? How many?

Patterns: Ladybugs come in special patterns, just like dinner plates. Compare your ladybugs. How many different patterns can you find?

Size: A ladybug is about the same size as a dried split pea. For fun, use split peas to figure out how many ladybugs would fit in a teaspoon, a cup, or in your hand.

Imagine yourself dressed for Halloween as none other than a giant ladybug. To get a preview of what you might look like, draw a picture of yourself in this special costume.

Trick-or-Treat Beetle

Questions, Anyone?: If you wonder about any weird parts you see as you draw your ladybug, jot down some questions, such as, What's that thing hanging down by its mouth, or What's that crack down its back? Your ladybug wonderings may lead to future discoveries.

Bigger than Life: You would be bigger—much bigger—than a real ladybug in your costume. Make your final drawing large. Fill most of the paper. For fun, add some other trick-or-treaters.

Art Show: Dazzle your family and friends with your new creation. Display your picture at the local art museum or neighborhood library, or on the family fridge. Maybe you'll even be a ladybug next Halloween!

You will need:

✔ paper
✔ a pencil
✔ an eraser
✔ watercolors, colored pencils, or crayons
✔ a ladybug

Look closely at your ladybug as you try each of the following activities.

Design Ideas: Like a real costume designer, make some quick, sloppy sketches of your ladybug to figure out the basic shape of the costume and all the parts that will be included.

Color Survey: What colors will you need for your costume? If you're using watercolors, you might try mixing paints to see if you can match the colors of your ladybug.

Do you have any ladybug questions? Here are some questions that kids in my town asked:

Why are ladybugs red? Why do they have spots? Do male and female ladybugs have the same number of spots? Are all ladybugs orange or red?

Do ladybugs have ears? Do they have feelers? How many eyes do they have? How many hearts?

What do ladybugs eat? How do they eat? What eats ladybugs? How fast can ladybugs walk? How fast can they fly? Can they swim? Can they jump? Do they like to walk up or down? How high can they fly? How far do they migrate?

Are there male ladybugs? How do ladybugs attract mates? When do they reproduce? Where do they lay their eggs? How many eggs do they lay? How do ladybugs react to heat? What do they do when they get cold? How strong are their shells? Do they mind bright light? How long do they live? How many different kinds of ladybugs are there?

Are you ready to explore unknown territory? Are you prepared to poke into mysteries? If you are, all you need to do is hold on to a ladybug question. Is there something you really wonder about ladybugs? Yes? Well, let that question lead you on a journey. Below are some tips for questioning ladybugologists.

Follow That Question

—Scrutinize: Could you answer your question through closer observation? For example, if your question was, "Do they have feet?" do you think you might be able to find feet by looking at a ladybug through a magnifying lens?

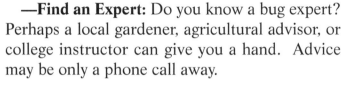

—Find an Expert: Do you know a bug expert? Perhaps a local gardener, agricultural advisor, or college instructor can give you a hand. Advice may be only a phone call away.

—Research: Other ladybugologists may have already explored your question. Perhaps the answer to your question lies in a book. It may even be in this one. If you don't find the answer somewhere in this book, look at some other books. If that doesn't work, you may need to experiment—read on.

—Experiment: Questions often lead to experiments. Could you answer your questions with an experiment? The chapter starting on page 36 called Kid Experiments has stories about experiments conducted by other bold ladybugologists. They may inspire you to be creative and set up your very own experiment.

Look at this ladybug. Can you find eyes, a nose, or a mouth? Can you find legs, wings, or feet? Do ladybugs have any body parts that are different from yours?

Ladybug Bodies

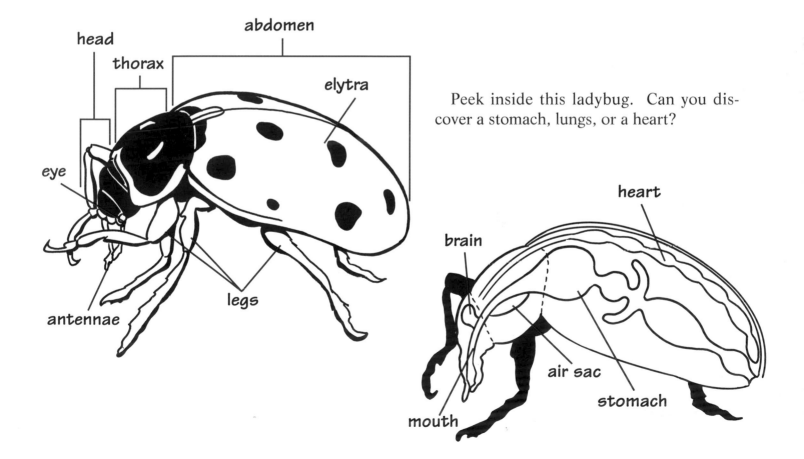

head

thorax

abdomen

elytra

eye

antennae

legs

Peek inside this ladybug. Can you discover a stomach, lungs, or a heart?

heart

brain

air sac

stomach

mouth

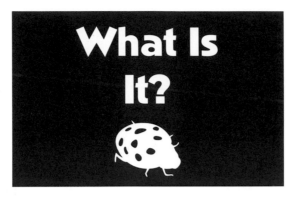

What Is It?

What is spotted like a leopard but lays eggs like a blue jay? What eats like a lion but sleeps in the winter like a bear? What protects itself like a poisonous frog but flies like a firefly? Would you believe—a ladybug? Ladybugs have similarities to all these animals, but their closest relatives are bees, beetles, and flies.

If you have examined ladybugs closely, you may have noticed that they have six legs. Ladybugs are insects, and all insects have six legs. Like other insects' bodies, the ladybug's body is divided into three sections: the head, **thorax,** and **abdomen.**

A ladybug's head is round and hard. The thorax in the middle is where an adult ladybug's three pairs of legs and two pairs of wings are attached. Ladybugs have an inner pair of wings, used for flying, and an outer pair. The **elytra** (EH-luh-truh), or outer pair of wings, are hard like a shell. These outer wings act like a sheath, or covering, to protect the ladybug. Ladybugs are part of the group of animals called **Coleoptera** (koh-lee-OP-teh-rah), which means "sheath wing." A ladybug's abdomen, or end section, is covered by the wings, but you can see it if you turn a ladybug over on its back.

All insects belong to a larger group of animals called **arthropods.** *Arthro* means "joint" and *pod* means "foot." All arthropods have jointed feet. Centipedes, shrimp, daddy longlegs, and sow bugs are all arthropods and distant cousins of the ladybug.

Check out your ladybug and your ladybug drawings. Does your ladybug fit the description of a Coleoptera, an insect, and an arthropod?

Arthropods are creatures with pairs of jointed legs. The animals below are arthropods.

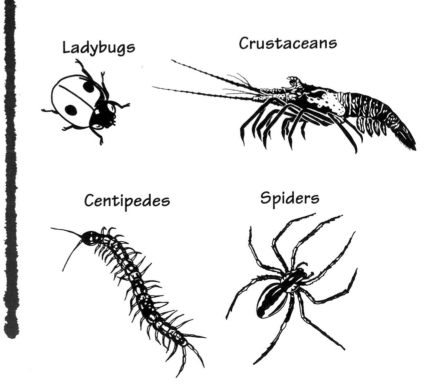

Ladybugs

Crustaceans

Centipedes

Spiders

Insects are arthropods with three body parts and three pairs of legs. The animals below are insects.

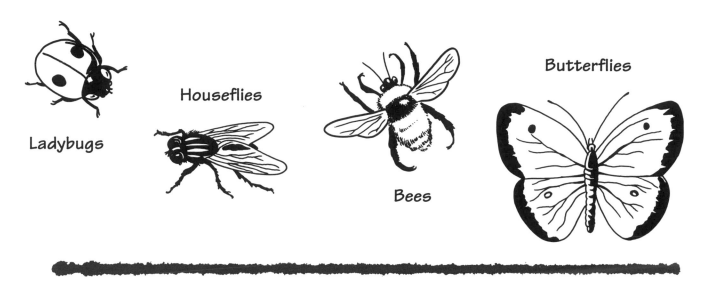

Ladybugs

Houseflies

Bees

Butterflies

Coleoptera are insects with a hard pair of outer wings. The animals below are Coleoptera.

Ladybugs

Ground Beetles

Fireflies

Longhorn Beetles

Each language has its own name for ladybugs. In Polish the word for ladybug is *biedronka*. In Danish the word is *mariehøne*. In Zulu it's *isilkazana esincane*. How do scientists from different countries talk to each other about the little red creature?

Biedronka, Mariehøne . . . Say What?

To avoid using a variety of names for plants and animals, scientists have devised a worldwide system for naming all living things. Whether you live in Poland, Denmark, or South Africa, each **species,** or kind, of ladybug has just one scientific name.

Latin and Greek, the ancient languages of Rome and Greece, are used in creating scientific names. Most kids already know a few scientific names, because dinosaurs are known by the names given to them by scientists. For example, *Ankylosaurus* is composed of the Greek words *ankylo* (crooked, bent) and *saurus* (lizard). The scientific name for the two-spotted ladybug is *Adalia* (grouping) *bipunctata* (two-spotted), because these ladybugs gather in large groups in the winter and they have two spots.

Other species of ladybugs may have many spots or, like the California ladybug, no spots at all. The yellow-spotted ladybug may have stripes or spots, and some Australian ladybugs are covered with splotchy markings. The polished ladybug is pale yellow with many black spots. Ladybugs also come in different sizes. The smallest are the size of a pinhead, while the largest are as big as a chocolate chip. Since there are more than two thousand species of ladybugs in the world, getting to know them all could take a while.

Aiolocaria hexaspilota

*Rodalia
limbata*

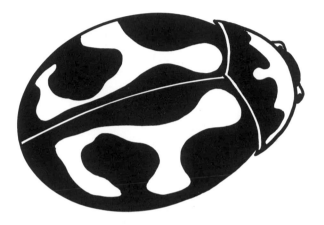

*Rodalia
cardinalis*

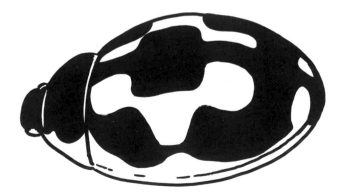

Propylea japonica

Ladybugs have had many names throughout time. In India, they were called Indra's cowherds after the goddess Indra. In England, they have been known as God's little cows or cow ladies, and in France, cows of the Lord. In Sweden, ladybugs are sometimes called Virgin Mary's golden hens. The American name for the bug—ladybug—is also thought to refer to Mary, the mother of Jesus, or "Our Lady." Ladybugs have also been called ladyflies, ladycows, and ladybirds.

In the old days, ladybugs were used to predict the future. In England, people believed they were a sign that crops would be plentiful. Folks in

Ladybug Lore

Central Europe thought that ladybugs meant good weather was on its way. When a ladybug crawled over a young woman's hands, she would say, "The ladybug measures me for my wedding gloves." This ladybug visit was supposed to guarantee a husband within a year.

Not only were ladybugs thought useful for farming and romance, but many people also thought they were a great cure for toothaches. Ladybugs were crushed, then stuffed into cavities. This was rumored to bring instant relief!

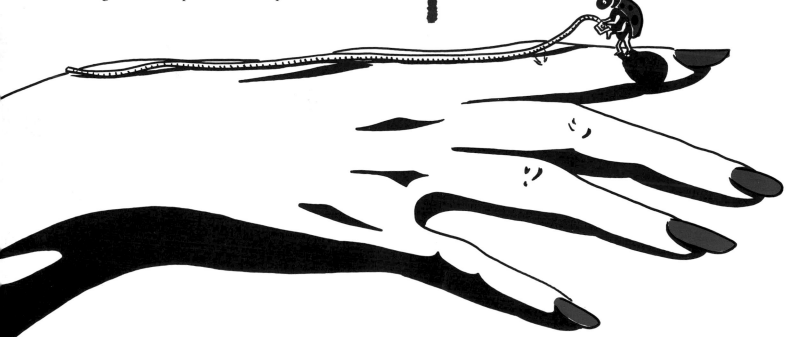

Even though their name makes it sound as if they are all female, a large number of the ladybugs you find will be male. Some people think that spotted ladybugs are females and unspotted ones are males, but this isn't the case.

It is a common sight to see one ladybug on the back of another. When they are examined from afar, it is hard to tell the difference between the two. But examination through a microscope will show that the ladybug getting a piggyback ride is a male.

Like other male insects, the male ladybug has a special organ, called an **aedeagus** (EE-dee-ah-gus), through which he delivers **sperm** to the eggs of the female. The sperm **fertilize** the eggs, which makes them able to grow. To mate, a male ladybug must climb up on a female ladybug's back. He may remain there for a few hours or even a few days, until mating is completed. A young female ladybug will be ready to mate within a few days of becoming an adult. Most females mate several times during their lifctime.

Once the female's eggs are fertilized by a male, she will lay from two to fifty eggs. Mother ladybugs do not stay around to take care of their young, but they do lay their eggs near the food that the young need to grow big and strong.

Like many other insects, ladybugs go through some major changes as they grow to be adults. Ladybugs begin their lives inside tiny orange or yellow eggs the size of poppy seeds. Female ladybugs deposit these eggs on leaves, on stems, or in bark crevices, and little six-legged orange-and-black larvae hatch from the eggs. These young ladybugs look very different from adult ladybugs. They are long, with narrow tail ends. They don't have the shiny wings of adult ladybugs, and they are splotched rather than dotted. Newly hatched larvae are at their first **instar,** or stage of growth.

After resting for up to a day on their eggshells, the ladybug larvae set out to look for food. They are so hungry, they will eat anything they can get in their jaws, including their brothers and sisters. On a steady diet of little creatures, such as tiny bugs called **aphids** (AY-fehdz), the larvae (seen in photo on right) grow and grow and grow.

Soon the ladybug larvae become so fat, they look as if they will burst. At this time, their skin actually splits and peels off. This process of shedding skin is called **molting.** Once the larvae have molted, they are soft and able to puff out their bodies. Soon after swelling up to a larger size, their new skin hardens. A larva that has molted once is at its second instar. Ladybug larvae usually molt four times, and they have four instars.

Shape Changers

Ladybugs are larvae for one to five weeks, depending on the temperature. The warmer the temperature, the faster the larvae grow. When a larva reaches full size, it is soon ready to change its shape. A larva glues itself to a leaf or other safe location, then sheds its skin for the fourth time.

From the skin emerges an orange-and-black **pupa** (PYOO-pah). The pupa is covered by a shell that looks like a legless ladybug. Inside, the pupa is slowly changing into an adult. If touched, the pupa will wiggle, but it cannot go anywhere.

After three to fifteen days, an adult ladybug will climb out of the pupal shell. These adult beetles look so different from the larvae that many people can't believe they are the same creatures. Along with its elytra (hard outer wings), an adult ladybug has a set of underwings used for flight. These underwings are clear. The elytra of freshly emerged adults are light orange and without dots, and the tips of their inner wings stick out from underneath. Within a few hours, dots appear on the elytra and the lower wings are fully tucked under, but the wing color may remain light for months. This makes it easy to tell new adult ladybugs from older ones.

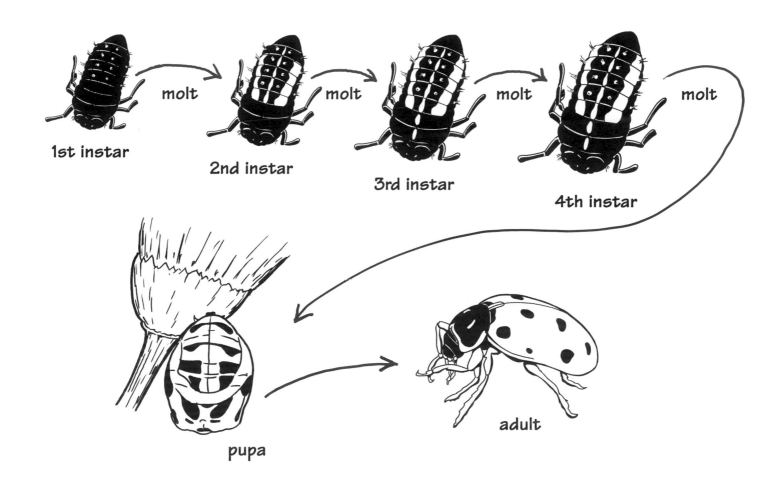

1st instar

molt

2nd instar

molt

3rd instar

molt

4th instar

molt

pupa

adult

You've probably seen herds of cows grazing in meadows, but have you ever seen herds of sap-drinking aphids grazing on leaves? These tiny insects look like water bags with legs and **antennae.** Using needle-like beaks, aphids tap into the sap surging through the stems and leaves of plants. The sap pours in so fast that aphids would blow up like balloons if they didn't release partly digested sap from their back ends. This sweet, sticky sap left behind by aphids is called honeydew. Honeydew is sticky because, like soda pop, it's full of sugar.

Cows provide milk, but their meat may be used for hamburgers. Aphids are also eaten for their meat—it's bugburgers that ladybugs are in search of. An aphid is a perfect snack for a ladybug. Not only is it easy to catch, but it's filled with sweet sap. With its large jaws, a ladybug will

Terrors of Leaf Land

munch aphid after aphid until it is full. (You can see a lady-bug larva eating aphids in the photo below.) Adult ladybugs may eat as many as one hundred aphids per day. That's a lot of bugburgers!

Ladybugs also dine on tiny armored insects called scales that cover leaves and branches like billions of freckles. Ladybugs eat a variety of bugs, including mites, thrips, mealy-bugs, very young caterpillars, beetle larvae, and fly maggots. To all of these peaceful leaf munch-ers, ladybugs are the terrors of leaf land.

Though most ladybugs are meat eaters, some eat plants. The Mexican bean beetle, which is yel-low with sixteen black spots, can do serious dam-age to beans and clover. The squash beetle has fourteen black spots and eats pumpkins and other squashes.

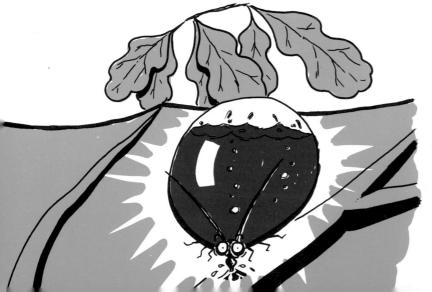

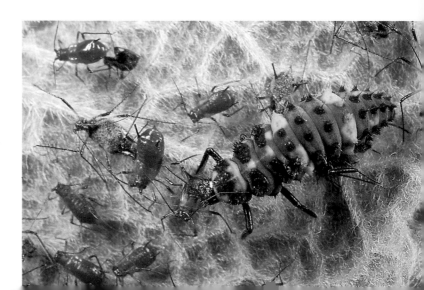

In the spring, aphid honey-dew can fall from the sky like rain. Living in trees, roses, and other plants are billions and billions of aphids. Aphids can reproduce, or have babies, very quickly. When female aphids are only six days old, they can give birth to baby aphids. With all these aphids being born, it's no wonder that plants can quickly be overrun by sap-drinking aphids.

A Plant's Best Friend

When people try to kill off aphids with poisons called **pesticides,** it may be only a few days before more aphids fly in from somewhere else. Meanwhile, the pesticides have also killed off ladybugs and other creatures that eat aphids. These predators, or hunters, can't expand their numbers as fast as aphids, so in the end, pesticides really help the aphids.

Long before pesticides were available, farmers depended on ladybugs for bug control. In the 1860s, California was home to many new orchards where oranges, lemons, and other citrus fruits were grown. The climate was perfect, and the farmers were successful—until a small plant-eating insect was accidentally brought in from Australia. This creature was called the cottony-cushion scale because of a white egg sac found on its back. Since it had no predators in California, the cottony-cushion scale spread quickly and killed large numbers of trees. Many farmers just gave up and left their citrus groves.

Fortunately, a clever ladybugologist named Albert Koebele came to the rescue. He searched in Australia for an insect that would eat the scale, and in 1892, he brought back a species of ladybug that dined on cottony-cushion scales and nothing else. Within a year, these ladybugs were heroes. They had saved the orange, grapefruit, and lemon groves. Since that time, ladybugologists have been carefully studying ladybugs to figure out better ways to control insects and other arthropods that eat crops.

Spotted Stop Signs

A red ladybug on a green leaf stands out like a spotted stop sign. Like a stop sign, the ladybug's red color may also be a warning marker. Hold a ladybug up to your nostrils and take a good whiff. Can you smell anything? Ladybugs give off a bitter odor. When ladybugs are found in large numbers, you can even smell them from a few feet away!

Experiments have shown that ladybugs probably aren't too tasty. Some birds, mammals, lizards, toads, and turtles will refuse to snack on ladybugs. Animals that try a ladybug once will usually stay away from them in the future. The bitter smell and bright red color of ladybugs may help remind animals not to have ladybugs for lunch.

Though ladybugs taste terrible to many critters, they are attacked by **parasites,** creatures that feed on living animals. Female parasitic wasps and flies drill holes into ladybug larvae, pupae, or adults, then lay eggs inside. When the eggs hatch, the worm-like wasp larvae begin to munch the ladybug's guts. By the time the wasp larvae change into

pupae, the ladybug is dead. The adult wasps or flies that come out of the cocoon then fly off in search of sweet nectar. Once adult parasites have eaten this high-powered fuel, they have the energy to search for mates and to lay more eggs—in ladybugs.

Ants also attack and sometimes kill ladybugs. Many species of ants feed on honeydew, and to these ants, a ladybug is like a wolf attacking their milk cows. When attacked by ants, most ladybugs will flee. But some species of ladybugs defend themselves by oozing a sticky substance that gums up the ants.

Ladybugs may also be killed off by diseases. In some years, as many as seven out of every ten ladybugs die before winter because of disease or parasites. The ladybugs that survive may reach one year of age, though some Asian ladybugs have lived to the ripe old age of three.

Ladybug, ladybug, fly away home,

Your house is on fire, your children will burn.

In the old days when farmers used fire to clear land for new crops, they would call out this warning to ladybugs. They knew the ladybugs were a help to them in controlling plant-eating insects and didn't want them to be toasted in the flames. Though ladybugs don't have homes like we do, many are found in the same **dormancy** (resting) sites from year to year.

Slumber Party Beetles

In spring and early summer of each year, ladybugs can usually find plenty of aphids and other small bugs to eat. But toward the end of summer, the bug cupboard may become a little bit bare. At this time, many species of ladybugs will fly to cooler locations, such as dark, moist forests or high mountains. The low temperatures in these places cause the ladybugs to slow down. Sloweddown ladybugs don't need to eat much, which helps them survive the winter, when little food is available.

Ken Hagen, a California ladybugologist, studied one species, the convergent ladybug, for many years. He found that convergent ladybugs living along the California coast store large amounts of fat in their bodies, like bears getting ready for winter. The ladybugs use this fat for food during a long winter rest.

Hagen also noticed that when most of the aphids have been eaten up in the fall, convergent ladybugs get ready to leave for better hunting grounds. In the mornings, when the air is still calm, the ladybugs fly straight up, riding the rising air currents. Soon they are so high that it is too cold for them to fly, so they drop into warmer air and fly once more. As they cruise along, they drift with the air currents.

Each day, the ladybugs are carried a little farther, until they reach the Sierra Nevada Mountains. Eventually, they find sunlit spots where they gather in large winter slumber parties. Hagen and other ladybugologists have found piles with as many as 40,000,000 ladybugs!

Ladybug slumber parties are truly cool. Cold winter temperatures chill ladybugs to the point that they can't move or eat. Unlike at a kid's slumber party, there isn't much action. The ladybugs just rest quietly through the winter, living off stored fat, until they are aroused by warmer temperatures. Then the convergent ladybugs ride the winds once more, but this time they travel back down the mountains to the valleys in the west.

Many other species of ladybugs throughout the world besides the convergent ladybug take off on long journeys to resting sites. The ten-spotted ladybug settles down for the winter in hills or mountains on large rocks, heaps of stones, posts, or shrubs. The seven-spotted ladybug prefers cozy resting spots under stones or leaves, or in holes in the ground. Two-spotted ladybugs are often found in bark crevices or cracks in buildings. In late fall, winter, or early spring, you can check out some of these locations. Perhaps you'll find some sleepy ladybugs. If you do, be a considerate neighbor and let them slumber until the warm days of spring.

The students at El Portal Elementary School, my local school in California, explored some of their ladybug questions by devising some fascinating and fun experiments.

Will Ladybug Larvae Go to Aphids?

Matteo, Rachel, and David watched two ladybug larvae that they had set in a container with some aphids. One larva walked onto the branch where the aphids were feeding. It passed near an aphid, then walked away. When the ladybug stopped for a while, Rachel thought it was napping. Matteo watched as the larger larva crawled onto the branch. It was heading right toward an aphid. Matteo thought it was going to eat the aphid, but the larva continued to wander around on the leaves. After a few minutes, the larva walked toward an aphid, then swung one of its legs back and forth. Next, the ladybug larva grabbed the aphid with its jaws and began to eat it. Within a couple of minutes, the aphid was completely munched up. Matteo was amazed.

David, Rachel, and Matteo decided that ladybug larvae will go to an aphid, but only when they get close enough to see it. What do you think an adult ladybug would do? Find one and place it with some aphids to see what happens!

What Plants Do Ladybugs Like?

Michelle, Candice, and Stephanie placed ladybugs on the sidewalk and arranged piles of flowers, leaves, and grass in a circle around them. After a while, some of the ladybugs crawled onto the flowers and some went to the grass. Michelle thought that since the ladybugs were crawling on the flowers and grass, they liked them. Do you agree? Why do you think ladybugs would go to grass or flowers?

In another test, Jamie and Josh wanted to see if ladybugs would eat leaves. They placed two ladybugs in a container with a pile of leaves. For fifteen minutes, they watched the ladybugs but didn't see them eat the leaves. They concluded that ladybugs don't like to eat leaves.

Will a Ladybug Fly Off a Pencil?

Allison wondered if ladybugs would fly when they reached the top of a pencil. After watching eleven different ladybugs climb her pencil, this is what she discovered:

Climbed down: 8
Flew Away: 3

Allison thought that the ladybugs may have climbed down because they couldn't see any place to fly to. Do you agree? When she repeated the test using a grass stem, she got mixed results. One ladybug stayed on top, one flew, one fell off, and one walked back down.

How Fast Can a Ladybug Climb?

Ali and Alex stood a yardstick on end, then placed a ladybug at the bottom. It marched right on up as Alex timed it with his watch. The ladybug reached the top in 31 seconds. Rhyen tried the same test, and his ladybug reached the summit in 53 seconds. At the faster rate, a ladybug could climb to the top of a one-hundred-story skyscraper in about three hours! How fast does your ladybug climb?

How Will Ladybugs Escape a Jar?

The thirty-seven ladybugs that Nathan collected in a jar crawled busily and acted like they wanted to get out. Nathan wondered what they would do when he let them go. Would they fly or simply walk away? When Nathan went outside to release them, Denise and Emily joined him to help tally the ladybugs' actions. It was not easy to keep track of the milling ladybugs, but Emily, Denise, and Nathan watched carefully and put tally marks on their data sheet. This is what they found out:

Flew Away: 19
Walked Away: 18

Why do you think some decided to fly and others chose to walk? Do you think you would get the same results?

Which Way Will Ladybugs Climb?

Rebecca wondered if ladybugs would climb horizontally or vertically. She taped two pencils together to make a cross. One at a time, she placed ladybugs on the bottom of the cross. Then she watched to see if they would walk straight to the top or turn off on one of the arms. Rebecca used nine different ladybugs and placed them on the cross five times each. Some ladybugs went mostly to the top, but some went on the arms more often.

Rebecca averaged her results and discovered that ladybugs will choose to go up to the top three out of five times. How do you think this behavior might help ladybugs as they hunt for food or mates?

Can Ladybugs Swim?

To test the swimming abilities of ladybugs, Chris and Josh placed three ladybugs in a container of water. To their surprise, they discovered that all three ladybugs could not only stay afloat, but they even paddled about. Ben, Matt, and Zack placed ladybugs in a pie tin filled with water and noticed that the ladybugs would paddle straight to the edge and climb out. However, when they placed the ladybugs in a jar full of water, the ladybugs were unable to swim to the edge. Though they kept paddling, they couldn't reach the wall of glass. Ben wondered why. What do you think?

In another set of swimming tests, Jeremy found that ladybugs can climb out of the water onto floating objects, such as twigs and leaves. He also discovered that they can swim even when they are upside down!

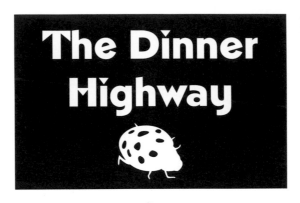

The Dinner Highway

Most of us don't have sharp-fanged jaguars prowling through our backyards, but we may have some spotted hunters searching for a tasty meal. A British ladybugologist, A. F. G. Dixon, has been studying the hunting behaviors of ladybugs for over thirty years. In the 1950s, Dixon did a series of experiments to discover how ladybugs find the aphids and other small bugs they hunt.

Which way will a ladybug larva go if you place it in the middle of an upright plant stem? Dixon placed larva after larva on stems and found that they almost always went up. He assumed that this behavior helped them reach the tops of branches, where the fresh new leaves (which aphids like) grow.

Dixon also watched ladybug larvae as they searched the undersides of leaves and kept notes on their exact routes. After many tests, he discovered that ladybugs used the veins and edges of leaves as trails. When Dixon examined feeding aphids, he found that they almost always fed near these veins and edges. To ladybugs, leaf veins and edges are highways to dinner.

Ladybugs are busy searchers. They follow stem after stem, vein after vein, until they encounter an aphid, mite, or other delicious bug. Dixon wondered if the number of prey in an area affected the way ladybugs hunted. To find out, he used an upright wooden stick that had measurements marked on it. On his stick, he placed some ladybug larvae that had been recently fed and others that had not had a meal for a while. As he watched the larvae, he kept track of the number of times they changed direction during their climbs up and down the stick.

After testing many ladybug larvae, Dixon found that well-fed larvae change direction often, like a kid who's "it" in a game of tag. This causes them to stay in a small area. Hungry ladybugs, on the other hand, turn less and search over a larger area, like a kid who's "it" in a game of hide-and-seek. This made sense to Dixon. Since aphids and other sap-sucking bugs often live in groups, a ladybug who has just eaten one of these bugs is likely to find another nearby if it keeps turning. Hungry ladybugs search over a larger area until they run into groups of bugs to munch. Once they have had a meal, they then patrol the immediate neighborhood for the rest of the bugs in the colony.

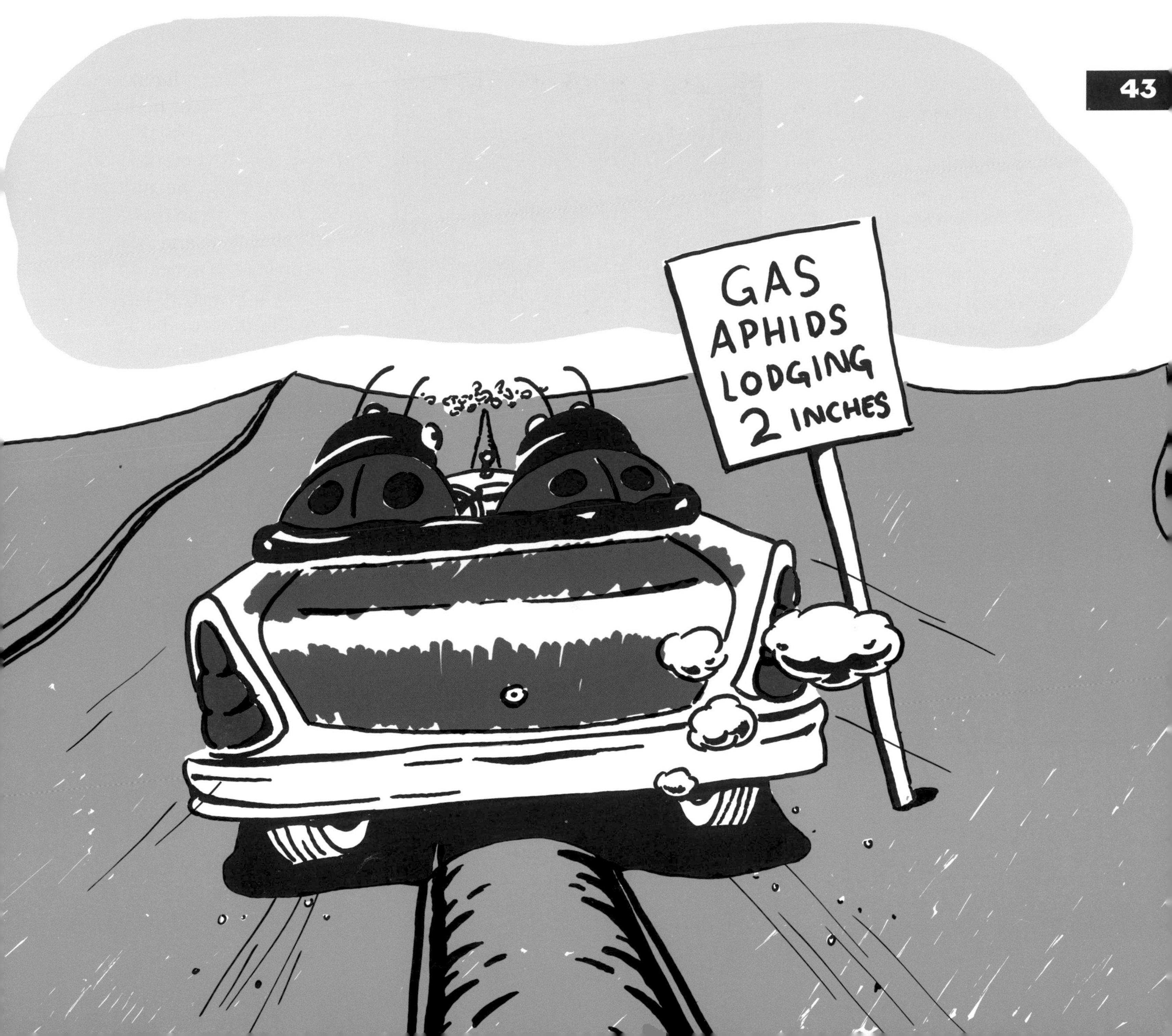
GAS
APHIDS
LODGING
2 INCHES

Although this is the end of the book, it is only the beginning of ladybugology. Remember those questions you jotted down? Are all of them answered? This book could probably not be big enough to answer all the ladybug questions—new questions are asked every day. Did you come up with some new questions as you investigated ladybugs? Maybe no one else has ever asked your questions.

As you have probably discovered, some questions are harder to answer than others. Although they can be frustrating,

Mysteries of a Backyard Buddy

challenging questions sometimes lead to the most exciting adventures. An easily explored question is like a short trip through a familiar place, while a real mystery is like an expedition to a strange and fantastic universe. Consider your unanswered questions once more and imagine the crazy investigations they could lead you into. What are you waiting for? Pack your gear and head out into question land.

Below are some questions that kids in my town may be pursuing at this very instant.

How high can ladybugs fly?

How strong are ladybug's shells?

How do ladybugs attract mates?

Why do they have spots?

Do they mind bright light?

How do they react to heat?

What leftover questions do you have?

Glossary

abdomen: the rear section of an insect's body

aedeagus: the male insect's sexual organ, used to insert sperm into females

antennae: sense organs found on the heads of certain animals, such as insects

aphids: small insects that drink plant sap

arthropods: a large group of animals with jointed legs and segmented bodies

Coleoptera: a group of insects with hard outer wings that includes ladybugs, fireflies, and other beetles

dormancy: a period of sleep or rest

elytra: the hard, shieldlike outer wings of a beetle

fertilize: to cause an egg to develop

instar: a stage of growth in a larva's development

larvae: young insects in an early stage of development

molting: the shedding of skin, fur, or feathers

parasites: animals that live on or in another animal and depend upon it for food

pesticides: chemicals used to kill insects and other animals

prey: animals that are hunted and eaten by others

pupa: the stage of an insect's life in which it changes from a larva into an adult

species: a group of animals with common traits, especially the means of creating young

sperm: the fluid that fertilizes a female's eggs

thorax: the middle section of an insect, where legs or wings may be attached

Index

About the Author

For over twenty years, Michael Elsohn Ross has taught visitors to Yosemite National Park about the park's wildlife and geology. Mr. Ross, his wife, Lisa (a nurse who served nine seasons as a ranger-naturalist), and their son, Nick, have led other families on wilderness expeditions from the time Nick learned to crawl. Mr. Ross studied conservation of natural resources at the University of California/Berkeley, with a minor in entomology (the study of insects). His other books for children include the Naturalist's Apprentice series, also published by Carolrhoda.

Mr. Ross makes his home on a bluff above the wild and scenic Merced River, at the entrance to Yosemite. His backyard garden is a haven for rolypolies, crickets, snails, worms, caterpillars, ladybugs, and a myriad of other intriguing critters.

LARRY JOHNSON

King of the Court

BY BILL GUTMAN

MILLBROOK SPORTS WORLD
THE MILLBROOK PRESS
BROOKFIELD, CONNECTICUT

Photographs courtesy of NBA Photos: cover (Nathaniel
Butler), pp. 28 (Nathaniel Butler), 30 (Lou Capozzola), 31
(Converse Communications), 34–35 (Andrew D. Bernstein), 36
(Nathaniel Butler), 40 (Gregg Forwerck), 41 (Gregg Forwerck),
44 (Nathaniel Butler), 46 (Nathaniel Butler); *The Charlotte
Observer:* cover inset (Bob Leverone), pp. 38–39 (Diedra
Laird), 42 (Bob Leverone); Wide World: pp. 3, 18, 21, 24, 26,
33; *The Dallas Morning News:* pp. 4 (Ken Geiger), 8 (Ken
Geiger), 11 (Evans Caglage), 12 (William Snyder); *The Odessa
American:* pp. 15, 17.

Library of Congress Cataloging-in-Publication Data
Gutman, Bill.
Larry Johnson, king of the court / by Bill Gutman.
p.   cm.—(Millbrook sports world)
Includes bibliographical references and index.
Summary: A biography of basketball star Larry Johnson, from his
days on the University of Nevada at Las Vegas NCAA championship
team to his triumphs with the Charlotte Hornets.
ISBN 1-56294-502-5
1. Johnson, Larry, 1969–   —Juvenile literature.   2. Basketball
players—United States—Biography—Juvenile literature.   3. National
Basketball Association—Juvenile literature.   [1. Johnson, Larry,
1969–   .   2. Basketball players.   3. Afro-Americans—Biography.]
I. Title.   II. Series.
GV884.J634G88   1995
796.323′092—dc20   [B]   94-21817   CIP   AC
Published by The Millbrook Press, Inc.
2 Old New Milford Road
Brookfield, Connecticut 06804

LARRY JOHNSON

The Dixon Circle housing projects in South Dallas, Texas, overlook Green Bay Park. There was just one basket at the park, although there were often groups of boys playing there. But basketball wasn't the only activity in the neighborhood. It was a rough place where many drug dealers operated. The kids who lived there often fell victim to drugs and crime. Staying clean wasn't easy.

There was a time, however, in the mid-1980s when a big teenager drew a crowd whenever he went onto the court at Green Bay Park. In fact, he was usually there playing from morning to night. And the tougher the games became, the better he played. He would shoot over taller players. He would drive to the hoop through a crowd. He would rebound better than anyone.

Then one day he did something that astounded even his closest friends. Larry Johnson was in the midst of another heated game. At one point, he pounded the ball inside and went to the basket. As usual, he soared high in the air and, to make the point, slammed the ball through the hoop. Only this time he pounded it through with such force that the entire rim was literally ripped from the backboard.

*The power of the young Larry Johnson is obvious
as he slams the ball home in this photo taken during
his high school days. Dunks like this sometimes tore
the rim from the backboard at Green Bay Park.*

His good friend Greg Williams remembers. "It was the most impressive thing he ever did. The basket came right off the backboard in his hands. The little kids, you should have seen them screaming. Even though it ruined the court for a few days, it was an amazing thing to see. "In fact, people still talk about it all the time. It's amazing Larry didn't get hurt, with all that iron and all that force. But he just stood there at the end, holding the rim in his hand."

Larry's basketball skills and his strength were already legendary in the ghetto of South Dallas. But perhaps the most amazing thing about Larry Johnson was the tremendous respect everyone had for him. The drug users and drug dealers never pressured him to join them. On the contrary, they encouraged him to continue his pursuit of basketball. And when something dangerous was going down, they would warn him to leave.

"Those guys just didn't bother us," his friend Greg Williams said. "I think they just respected Larry. They'd even say, 'Hey, you'd better get out of here' when they were doing the bad stuff—the drinking, the gambling, whatever. They just didn't want him to be part of it."

Something was special about Larry Johnson even then. Drug dealers had no way of knowing that they were protecting a youngster who would become the Player of the Year in high school, win the same award at junior college and again at the University of Nevada at Las Vegas. From there he would be the top draft choice of the National Basketball Association, and soon after its Rookie of the Year.

Larry Johnson has never stopped reaching for and achieving new heights. Yet none of it would ever have happened if he hadn't first defeated the "War Zone," the mean streets of South Dallas.

A DIFFICULT CHILDHOOD

Larry Johnson was born on March 14, 1969, in Tyler, Texas. Tyler was also the home of another very famous athlete, pro Football Hall of Fame running back Earl Campbell. As a young boy, Larry remembers riding his bicycle past the trailer where Campbell grew up. Next to the trailer was the mansion Campbell built for his mother when he became an NFL star. Larry saw that, too.

Dortha Johnson was raising her son as a single parent. Young Larry had lots of friends and began playing sports. He was always bigger and stronger than the other boys his age. When he was nine he quarterbacked a Pop Warner League football team. All the other players were 14. He also began to box with the Police Athletic League in Tyler about that time. It was a sport that he would continue for five years and one that would toughen him up for the move to South Dallas.

That move came when he was 12. His mother went to work as a cook at an elementary school, and Larry had to fend for himself on the streets. At first he was tempted to follow some of the other boys he met. He and his friends stole bicycles and sometimes groceries. One day the police caught him and drove him to the station. There were no charges filed, but his mother didn't pick him up until late that night. She wanted him to learn a lesson, which he did.

It also didn't take Larry long to learn what life was really like in South Dallas. "It's one of the most messed-up areas I've ever seen," he says, even now. "You had your crack dealers, your cocaine dealers, your dopeheads, and police raids every night."

As a teenage basketball player in Texas, Larry was a boy in a man's body. He was already able to dominate a game with his size (a hint of which can be seen in his hands), strength, and talent.

Pretty soon, however, Larry was spending most of his time playing basketball. There was so much crime going on around the court at Green Bay Park that the boys often wondered if they would be hit by a stray bullet. And the games were rough and tough.

"You would have a fight a week," Larry remembers. "If you played Monday through Saturday and didn't have a fight, you knew you had to be ready for Sunday because you'd surely have a fight then."

By the time Larry was in the seventh grade there weren't too many boys who wanted to fight him. By that time he stood 6 feet 2 (188 centimeters) and weighed 190 pounds (86 kilograms). He was a boy who already had a man's body.

As Larry grew older, basketball became the main part of his life. He played constantly, ignoring the violence on the streets. His mother worried about him, but at least she always knew where he was.

"No matter how late it was I would just look out the window and there he was," Dortha Johnson said. "He'd be playing basketball. Always basketball."

As Larry continued to play basketball and turn his back on alcohol and drugs, the respect for him in the neighborhood grew. In a strange kind of way, those who knew that they themselves would never make it wanted him to make it.

"Those guys were bad," Larry has said of the drug dealers. "I knew it. But they always wanted me to do good."

HIGH SCHOOL SENSATION

By the time Larry was ready for high school, he was already a player who could dominate a game. Lincoln High, his neighborhood school, was an all-black school with many of the same problems that existed on the streets.

One of Larry's junior high school coaches suggested to his mother that Larry would be better off at Skyline High. It was a racially mixed school on the other side of the city. Dortha thought about it and decided to send her son to Skyline. To get there, Larry had to take the city bus and transfer twice along the way.

"I was known as the kid from South Dallas," Larry said. "Skyline was a place totally different from what I knew. They called it the Skyline Fashion Show. There were all these kids with all kinds of clothes. It was like a miniature college. But I didn't know anyone. Not until basketball started."

Although he was only in the ninth grade, Larry already felt he could play basketball with nearly anyone. As soon as practice started he walked up to the coach, J. D. Mayo, and told him he was good enough to play on the varsity.

At first, the coach just smiled. Ninth-graders didn't come in and play with the varsity right away. As the teams began to practice, Larry kept pestering the coach. There were three games scheduled for the first day of the season. The freshmen played first, then the junior varsity, and finally the varsity. Larry started for the freshmen and played well. The coach reconsidered. "Just before the varsity game started I suddenly had an idea," Coach Mayo said. "I thought, why don't I start the kid just to see how good he really is."

So Larry started for the varsity and immediately caught fire. During the first half he hit all eight shots from the field and one from the foul line. With 17 points already, Larry sought out Coach Mayo and asked, "How am I doing?"

"If you keep your great attitude and keep working hard," the coach said, "you'll be fine."

That was an understatement. Larry was better than fine. He was a dominant player and a star from his first game. Coach Mayo would later admit that Larry was "as good as he said he was."

At Skyline High, Larry speeds down the court in a 1986 game against Bishop Dunne High School. Even at this age, Larry's ball-handling was impressive.

Skyline High didn't lose a home game for the four years that Larry Johnson played. During that time he continued to practice relentlessly. After games, he went over to the local recreation center and played more basketball. He never seemed to get enough of the game.

By the time Larry finished his junior year, J. D. Mayo told Dortha Johnson something that he had never said to a parent before or since. He told her that Larry had a great chance to be an NBA player.

"He knew what he wanted, and he had the body to get it," Coach Mayo said. "I told his mother that if he takes care of business, he'll be a household name someday."

In his senior year Larry was simply outstanding. He was nearly 6 feet 5 (196 centimeters), well over 200 pounds (91 kilograms), and one of the very best high school players in the country.

Although he had terrific all-around skills, Larry's powerful inside game was what set him apart. Here he outmuscles two defenders to score during a high school game in 1987.

In fact, he is still remembered as the most dominating player in Dallas schoolboy basketball history. He often brought the crowds to their feet with rim-rattling dunks. He outrebounded much taller opponents and handled the ball as well as smaller guards. In one game against Dallas Jesuit, he led his team to a victory without taking a single shot. "He wanted to prove to everyone that we weren't a one-man team," said Coach Mayo.

THE LONG ROAD TO UNLV

It wasn't surprising that Larry's great basketball skills brought interest from many top colleges. What they didn't know then was that Larry was a very poor reader. It held him back in some of his classes. All high school students who want to go to college must take the Scholastic Aptitude Test (SAT). When Larry took the test his total score was below 700. That meant he would not be able to play basketball as a freshman at a four-year college.

At that time, Larry had just about decided to attend Southern Methodist University (SMU) in Dallas. So he took the SAT once more. This time his score was above 700. Then the university decided that it wanted him to take the test a third time, to be sure. Larry felt he shouldn't have to do this. The second test should have been enough.

At this point, Larry did some serious thinking. He didn't want to miss a year of basketball, but he also knew that he had some catching up to do with his reading skills. That would be tough to do with the pressure of big-time basketball. So instead of SMU, he decided to attend Odessa Junior College in Odessa, Texas.

Larry graduated from Skyline High in June 1987, and enrolled that fall at Odessa. Located in West Texas, Odessa had once been a thriving oil town. But the wells had long since dried up. Now sports was the thing that got people in Odessa excited.

As soon as they saw the nearly 6-foot-7 (201-centimeter), 230-pound (104-kilogram) freshman in action, Odessa had a new hero. Larry Johnson was the best thing to happen to the town since the wells were discovered. As one local writer described Larry, "He can run like a deer and pound like a bull, with hands as soft as his smile and a work ethic as genuine as his personality."

For two years Larry dazzled the Odessa fans with his incredible, all-around play. During his freshman year he averaged 22 points and 18.1 rebounds a game. Odessa had a winning season, and Larry was named the nation's top freshman player by both *The Sporting News* and the *Basketball Times*. Shortly after that he was named Junior College Player of the Year.

In addition, without the pressure of big-time college basketball, Larry was able to concentrate on his studies and had already increased his reading level dramatically.

Back on the court for the 1988–1989 season, he was better than ever. He was strong and muscular, his weight beginning to approach the 250-pound (113-kilogram) mark. Yet he lost none of his quickness or leaping ability. It wasn't long before he began putting together some truly remarkable games.

Larry was a force at Odessa Junior College right from the beginning. On defense he was tough to go around and rebounded as well as anybody.

Against Midland he had 39 points and 22 rebounds. In another contest he burned the hoop to the tune of 51 points. In yet another he moved from power forward to small forward and promptly hit 41 points, including five shots from 3-point range. Those who saw him lead the Odessa fast break said he handled the ball well enough to play point guard.

Head coach Dennis Helms was always one of Larry's biggest boosters. He remembered the Midland game when Larry had picked up his third foul. Some players would let up, fearful of fouling out. Not Larry.

"He immediately intercepts a pass," the coach recalled, "dribbles down the floor, and goes one-on-one against a guy who is trying to stop him. So he takes off outside the foul lane with both feet, reaches out and dunks, gets fouled intentionally, makes both free throws, and we get the ball out of bounds."

When the season ended, Odessa had a 33–2 record and won the regional title. Larry averaged 28.3 points and 17.3 rebounds a game. For the second straight year he was named Junior College Player of the Year. People were already calling him the best college player in the country at any school.

Larry knew that it was time to move on, but he also saw the value of his junior college experience. For one thing, his reading level was now where it should be.

"I loved junior college," he said. "I look at my classes at Odessa and I know I couldn't have kept up my grades coming right out of high school. I tell other guys in my shoes not to go to a four-year school. Do it the way I did."

Larry was saying that at a junior college he could compete in basketball and also concentrate on his studies without a lot of added pressure. Now he was prepared to transfer to a four-year school.

There wasn't a school in the country that would turn Larry down now. One of the schools that wanted him badly was the University of Nevada at Las Vegas (UNLV). The Runnin' Rebels were 29–8 the year before and one of the better teams in the country. With all their starters returning, the feeling was that if they added Larry Johnson they could go all the way.

Larry was interested in UNLV, but what helped him decide was his newfound friendship with Greg Anthony and Stacey Augmon. Anthony and Augmon were UNLV starters and had met Larry at the 1988 Olympic Games trials. Their enthusiasm convinced Larry to attend Nevada–Las Vegas in the fall of 1989.

When Larry goes inside to the hoop, defenders move out. He once scored 51 points for Odessa in a single game.

RUNNIN' REBEL SUPERSTAR

With the addition of Larry Johnson, UNLV had a powerful team. Greg Anthony was an outstanding point guard, while Anderson Hunt had All-American potential at shooting guard. Augmon was the small forward and an outstanding two-way player. David Butler and George Ackles would probably share the center spot. Larry would move in at power forward, making the Rebels an immediate preseason top-ten pick.

"I'm really looking forward to playing with these guys," Larry said. "I watched them on television several times last year and love the way they play. Whether I start or come off the bench, I know I'll fit in."

There was no way, of course, that Larry Johnson would be on the bench.

Larry was soon leading the Runnin' Rebels in scoring and rebounding.

He was too strong and too talented for that. Although some UNLV fans thought of Larry as a savior, he looked at himself as just another piece to a puzzle.

"The pressure won't be on me," he said. "It will be on the entire team."

The team quickly showed it was a force. Larry fitted like a glove, becoming the Rebels' top scorer and rebounder almost from the first game. His unselfishness and leadership abilities made him popular with his teammates and the coach, Jerry Tarkanian. UNLV got off quickly and was indeed a top-ten team all year.

Reserve guard Stacey Cvijanovich spoke for many when he said, "I've never seen anyone like Larry. I've never played with anyone as good as he is. There are a lot of gifted athletes on this team, but Larry is the cream of the crop."

Coach Tarkanian simply called Larry "the best player we ever recruited."

And shooting guard Anderson Hunt put it this way: "Last year, we needed that one person who could just give us a basket anytime we needed it. Now we have him. I knew he was the man from the first time I played with him."

The Rebels were tough to beat during the season. Coming into the NCAA tournament they had lost just five games. Those losses were in the first half of the season, and many now thought that UNLV would win the national championship. The Rebels were the top seed in the West Regional. They opened with a 102–72 win over Arkansas–Little Rock, then beat Ohio State, and next won a close one against Ball State, 69–67. Now they had to face Loyola Marymount of California. The winner would go to the Final Four.

Loyola was the highest-scoring team in the country. They were a run-and-gun ballclub, and some thought that the Rebels would play a slow-down game against them. But Coach Tarkanian said otherwise. "I expect 40 minutes of full-court basketball," he told the press.

The game really served to show what an all-around powerhouse the Runnin' Rebels had become. They simply beat Loyola at their own game. Not only did they beat them; they destroyed them. At the half it was 67–47, and when it ended the Rebels had a 131–101 victory and a trip to the Final Four.

Against Loyola the team looked awesome. Augmon had 33 points, while Anderson Hunt added 30 with 13 assists. Larry had 20 points and scrubbed the boards with 18 rebounds. Greg Anthony also scored 20 and missed just two shots. They were the favorite to take it all.

In the semifinals, Duke defeated Arkansas, 97–83. Then UNLV met Georgia Tech, led by slick point guard Kenny Anderson and the sharp-shooting Dennis Scott. With those two playing brilliantly, the Yellow Jackets raced to a 53–46 halftime lead. But after intermission, the balanced attack of UNLV wore Georgia Tech down.

It started with a 10–1 run at the outset of the second half. That gave the Rebels the lead at 56–54. From there they slowly stretched it out,

Larry scored 22 points in the 1990 NCAA semi-final game against Georgia Tech. One game later the Rebels were national champions.

winning 90–81, to reach the finals against Duke. Larry and his teammates could now taste a national championship. They came out for the final with fire in their eyes, took an early lead, and never looked back.

The Rebels made 10 of their first 14 shots and opened up a 21–11 lead. It was 47–35 at the half, and it only got better for the Rebels. They ran, shot, rebounded, and defensed their way to a 103–73 victory. They had won the national title with the greatest margin of victory in NCAA finals history. Hunt led the way with 29 points, while Larry scored 22 and grabbed 11 rebounds.

"This is the greatest," Larry said after the game. "But no single player deserves more credit. It has been a real team effort all year."

That was true. Hunt, Anthony, and Augmon were all great players in their own right. The bench was also tough. But it was the addition of Larry Johnson that put the team over the top. In 40 games, Larry scored 822 points for an average of 20.6 a game. He had a 62.4 shooting percentage and also grabbed 457 rebounds, an average of 11.4 per game.

After the season, he became a consensus first-team All-American selection, being named on all the major teams. In one year of college ball, Larry Johnson had already reached the absolute top.

PLAYER OF THE YEAR

There was some talk that Larry would enter the NBA draft after his junior season. The NCAA was investigating the UNLV program for violations of a number of NCAA rules, and for a while it looked as if the Rebels wouldn't be allowed to defend their national title. But the NCAA felt it wasn't fair to penalize the returning players. They decided to allow the Rebels to go to the NCAA tournament in 1990–1991. That's when Larry made his final decision to return.

With all the starters back, the Rebels were stronger than ever. They began rolling over opponents right from the beginning of the year. The team was so powerful that their opposing teams found many games out of reach before halftime. Johnson, Augmon, Anthony, and Hunt all looked like future NBA players. The Rebels were rolling through their season unbeaten.

"This is a team that could enter the NBA as is and win a lot of games," wrote one reporter. Many agreed. The Rebels just seemed too talented and too strong for the rest of the teams chasing them. During one six-game run in December, the Rebels won by margins of 20, 41, 50, 20, 34, and 32 points. It was hard to see any college team beating them.

The team was 19–0 and rated number one in the country when they met second-ranked Arkansas in a showdown game at Fayetteville, Arkansas. At the half, Arkansas had a 50–46 lead and Larry had just two baskets. But in the second half the Rebels rolled. A 29–11 run put them up 75–61, and the final was 112–105. Larry finished with 25 points and 14 rebounds, while Augmon led all scorers with 31 points.

When the regular season ended, the Rebels were 27–0 and the number one team in the country. Everyone expected them to run through the NCAA tournament and win another national title. After the conference tournaments, the Rebels were 30–0 and ready to defend their title.

First the Rebels routed Montana, 99–65, making it look easy. Next was a second-round game with Georgetown. Although Larry and the team

*By 1991, Larry was one of the most popular and well-known college players in
the country. Here he is besieged by fans at the Hoosier Dome in Indianapolis,
as the Rebels get ready to meet Duke in the NCAA semi-finals.*

took the lead from the start and held it, they could never quite put Georgetown away. The Hoyas kept coming back, cutting the lead at one point
from 15 to 4. When it ended, UNLV won, 62–54, but it was just the
second time all year that the team hadn't won by 10 points or more.

Then in the West Regional final, the Rebels defeated Seton Hall, 77–
65. Once more they didn't look overwhelming. But they were on their
way to the Final Four once again. Larry led the way with 30 points against
Seton Hall and was named the Most Outstanding Player in the Regional.

The team had now won 45 straight games, the fourth-longest winning streak in NCAA history. But not everyone was happy about the way they were playing.

"Our intensity has been incredible for most of the year, but right now it's not incredible," said Coach Tarkanian.

In their semifinal game, the Rebels had a rematch with Duke, the team they had overwhelmed for the national title a year earlier. The Blue Devils wouldn't be pushovers. They had an All-American in 6-foot-11 (211-centimeter) Christian Laettner and other fine players, such as Bobby Hurley, Thomas Hill, Brian Davis, and Grant Hill. They also had a plan. At the outset of the game they fronted Larry on defense, making it hard for him to get the ball. And when Duke was on offense, Laettner stayed outside, often taking Larry away from the boards. UNLV never really adjusted.

Duke took an early 15–6 lead. The Blue Devils continued to front Larry and double-team him. But the shooting of Hunt and Anthony brought Vegas back, and the Rebels took a 43–41 lead at the half.

The second half was again close. With 3 minutes and 51 seconds left and UNLV leading, 74–71, Anthony drove to the hoop. The whistle blew, and Anthony was charged with the foul. He had fouled out. With their point guard gone, UNLV struggled. A Hunt layup made it 76–71, but moments later Hurley, then Thomas Hill, hit three-pointers. The game was tied at 77–77 with less than a minute left.

Laettner was then fouled and with 12 seconds remaining hit both free throws. Duke led, 79–77. It seemed likely that the Rebels would go to Larry for the last shot. But when Larry got the ball he was closely guarded

and passed it back out to Hunt. Hunt's long shot before the buzzer clanged off the rim. Duke had won. The Rebels had been upset. They would not repeat as national champs.

Larry had just 13 points in the final. But he took only 10 shots, showing how well Duke defensed the Rebels. He led both teams with 13 rebounds, and for the second straight year was the leading rebounder in the tournament. But that did not make losing any easier. Duke went on to win the championship.

It had still been a great year. Larry averaged 22.7 points a game and 10.9 rebounds. That gave him a 21.6 scoring mark for his UNLV career, with 11.2 rebounds a game. He was once again a consensus All-American. Better yet, he was the winner of the James Naismith

Although Larry was double-teamed most of the way against Duke, he did manage to get past the Blue Devils' Christian Laettner for 2 of his 13 points. But Duke upset UNLV, 79–77, ending the Rebels' dream of two straight NCAA titles.

Award and the John Wooden Award, both given to the man considered the best college player of the year.

Larry Johnson had lived up to all the expectations. He was a communications major at Vegas and close to his degree, planning to work toward that in summer school. In four years at both Odessa and UNLV his teams were a combined 134–13. He was a winner.

NUMBER ONE ROOKIE

With the NBA draft approaching in June of 1991, there seemed to be a good chance that Larry would be the number one choice. But there were critics too. Larry had always been listed as 6 feet 7 (201 centimeters). Some said he was really 6 feet 6 (198 centimeters) or even a "tall" 6 feet 5 (196 centimeters). Some said that in the NBA he would be overmatched as a power forward.

None of that bothered Larry. He was confident in his ability, no matter where he played. The team that had the top pick in the 1991 draft was the Charlotte Hornets. The Hornets were an expansion team in 1988. The team won just 20 games that year and found improvement coming slowly. They needed franchise players.

Charlotte coach Allan Bristow scouted Larry and some other top prospects. He came away with the ultimate praise for the UNLV star.

"Larry Johnson doesn't have any weaknesses," the coach said. "I've been around a lot of great players in my life, and all of them had weaknesses. I can't think of a single weakness for Larry."

In June 1991, Larry became the top pick of the entire NBA when the Charlotte Hornets drafted him number one. Here Larry celebrates with former teammates Stacey Augmon (left) and Greg Anthony (center). Augmon was picked by the Hawks and Anthony by the Knicks later in the first round.

That clinched it. On draft day, the Hornets wasted no time in making Larry the number one pick in the entire league. All his work, all those hours on the court at Green Bay Park, all the practice at Odessa and at Nevada–Las Vegas had paid off. He was about to become a pro.

But there was one problem. Larry and his agent couldn't agree on a contract with the Hornets. He held out during the preseason as both sides tried to reach agreement. At one point, there were rumors that Larry was going to play in Europe. The Hornets said that the NBA salary cap allowed them to give Larry only a certain amount of money the first year.

With agents and lawyers involved, many top draft picks take a long time to sign. The players just want to play. It was the same with Larry.

"I'm ready to play," he said, as the season opener drew closer. "I was ready three or four months ago. Nothing has been as terrible as waiting to get into camp."

Then, just a few days before the season opened, the waiting ended. It was announced that Larry and the Hornets had agreed on a six-year contract worth close to $20 million. Larry would receive $1.9 million the first year, with the money going up each year after that. Everyone was happy that the wait was over.

"I'm really happy for Larry," said Jerry Tarkanian, his UNLV coach. "I think he'll be a great player for Charlotte, and I'm happy he is financially set for the rest of his life. It couldn't have happened to a nicer person."

As for Larry, he was happy just to be back on the court. "I don't feel like I'm in game shape," he said, "but the only way to do that is to get out there with the team. I feel I can play against the Celtics Friday night. I didn't want to miss the first game. My dream has always been to play in the NBA."

Coach Bristow also planned to use Larry. "We don't run a lot of plays on offense, so it won't be hard for him to learn," the coach said. "And we run a lot of pressure defense like he played at UNLV."

Once he was on the court it didn't take Larry Johnson long to earn everyone's respect. In the opener against the Celtics he played about half

Larry was an immediate success in the NBA. Although considered short at 6 feet 7 inches, his inside game was tough to stop on both offense and defense.

the game and scored 14 points. Then the next night, the team came home to the Charlotte Coliseum, where a packed house of 23,698 fans gave Larry a standing ovation.

That night against the Nets, Larry was outstanding. He scored 16 points and grabbed 18 big rebounds. Even though the Hornets lost, 116–108, he had proved that he belonged. In fact, he really showed everyone that he had the tools to become a superstar.

"It gets a little better each day," he said, after the Nets game. "Tonight was a hundred percent better than last night. Plus the fans have been great. When I was holding out, I read the fans were really upset. But that reception tonight was great. I love the city of Charlotte. Everyone has been very friendly."

The Hornets had a few other fine players, like 5-foot-3 (160-centimeter) point guard Tyrone "Muggsy" Bogues, shooting guard Kendall Gill, and the sharpshooting Dell Curry. But the team was still in just its fourth season and needed more balance and more quality players. However, it now had a cornerstone in Larry Johnson.

As Larry continued to play better and better, he was also getting used to his new wealth. He bought his mother a home in Dallas and gave his grandmother a new car. He also bought himself a house in Charlotte. But that wasn't all. He immediately made donations to Skyline High School and Odessa Junior College. In addition, he gave the Charlotte chapter of the United Way a check for $180,000.

Larry didn't give money to UNLV immediately. He thought Coach Tarkanian was being treated unfairly by the university during the NCAA investigation. His only gifts consisted of equipment for the training room. He was still a man of high principles.

In addition, Larry had a contract with Converse basketball shoes. He soon made a television commercial, and the legend of "Grandmama" was born. Donning a wig, glasses, and a frumpy dress, Larry became a slam-dunking "grandmother" who put other players to shame. He also

By playing his own "Grandmama" in a series of basketball shoe commercials, Larry became even more well known and popular.

played the Grandmama character in a television situation comedy and later made a second commercial. It takes a confident man to appear on national television dressed like a granny.

"It was a lot of fun," Larry said about the commercial. "But that's hard work too. It took two days to shoot, and I was getting impatient at times. But I realized they wanted to do it right, so I got over it."

As the season wore on, Larry went up against the NBA's best. He matched skill and muscle with the likes of Charles Barkley, Carl Malone, Charles Oakley, Xavier McDaniel, and the other top power forwards. He also challenged the big centers like Patrick Ewing, David Robinson, and Hakeem Olajuwon. Even against them he more than held his own. There was little doubt that he was already a force and would only get better.

The Hornets still weren't a winning team. They finished the 1991– 1992 season with their best record ever, but it was just 31–51, not good enough for the playoffs. Larry, however, had been everything everyone expected—and more. He wound up leading all NBA rookies with 1,576 points, a 19.2 average. He also grabbed 899 rebounds for an 11.0 average.

In addition, he broke a slew of team records and finished second in the Slam Dunk competition at the NBA All-Star Weekend. In a game against Minnesota in March, he had 24 points and 23 rebounds. But his biggest prize came after the season, when he was named NBA Rookie of the Year.

"It feels real good to be the first former UNLV player to win the Rookie of the Year Award," he said. "I've got to admit I became a little nervous the last month of the year when people said I had a chance to win it. But the trophy isn't staying in Charlotte. It's going back to Dallas with me, and I'm giving it to my mom."

As he had done at Skyline High, then at Odessa Junior College, and finally at UNLV, Larry Johnson once again emerged as a star.

A ONE-TWO PUNCH AND A HUGE PACT

When the NBA draft for 1993 came around, the Hornets drew the second pick. The Orlando Magic had the first choice and picked 7-foot-1 (216-centimeter) center Shaquille O'Neal of Louisiana State University. O'Neal was considered a surefire franchise player, a dominant center who would become a superstar NBA player quickly. And he did.

Shortly after being named NBA Rookie of the Year, Larry takes to the mike to joke with reporters as a new Fleer basketball card celebrating his rookie prize is unveiled.

However, the Hornets fared almost as well. They chose 6-foot-10 (208-centimeter) center Alonzo Mourning of Georgetown. Mourning was an All-American and another unselfish player who always thought of the team first.

Like Larry before him, Mourning held out in a contract dispute. He didn't join the Hornets until the season was already under way. But when he came in, the Hornets found they had a tough, tenacious player who was outstanding on both offense and defense. When Mourning teamed with Larry, the Hornets suddenly had not one, but two, outstanding franchise players. With their new one-two punch in the lineup, the Hornets became winners.

At mid-season, Larry was voted to represent the Eastern Conference as a starter in the NBA All-Star Game. He joined Michael Jordan, Shaquille O'Neal,

Larry soars high in the air for a slam dunk before the 1992 NBA All-Star Game. He finished second in the slam dunk contest. A year later Johnson was named a starter for the Eastern Conference in the 1993 All-Star Game.

and David Robinson as the only four first- or second-year players to start an All-Star Game in the last ten years.

In the game itself, Larry played just 16 minutes, getting 4 points and 4 rebounds. Some criticized Coach Pat Riley for not playing Larry more, since he was voted a starter. Riley preferred playing the veterans. But Larry didn't let that bother him. "I'm not worried," he said. "I'm a young player and there will be other All-Star Games. I'll be back."

When the 1992–1993 season ended, Charlotte had the best record in team history, 44–38. They were in third place in the Central Division of the Eastern Conference. Better yet, they were in the playoffs.

Larry had put together another great season. He led the team in scoring with a 22.1 average and in rebounding with a 10.5 per game mark. He played in all 82 games for the second straight season and led the NBA in minutes played, averaging 40.5 minutes a game. He scored a career high 36 points against Golden State on December 2, and after the season ended received second-team All-NBA honors.

In the playoffs, Charlotte upset the Boston Celtics, winning the best-of-five series, 3–1. Next they had to play the powerful New York Knicks. The Knicks were still too strong for the young Hornets and eliminated them in five games, 4–1.

But it had been a successful season, with the promise of more to come. The Hornets were now an up-and-coming team.

Larry showed his usual outstanding hand and foot skills in the 1993 playoff game against the Celtics.

Larry suffered a setback during the off-season when he learned he had a herniated disk in his back. He didn't need surgery, but the injury would leave him at less than full strength when the 1993–1994 season began. But the back injury wasn't the biggest news coming out of the Charlotte camp.

During the summer it was announced that the Hornets had given Larry a contract extension. It was a blockbuster, one that stunned even longtime followers of the NBA. The contract, added on to his present deal, would cover 12 years and be worth the staggering sum of $84 million. It was the largest total contract in sports history.

Besides the huge amount of money, the new contract showed how much the Hornets thought of Larry Johnson. They wanted him to remain the cornerstone of the franchise, their leader. He would only say he was extremely pleased with the deal and would be "happy to remain a Charlotte Hornet for the rest of my career."

Larry gets a hug from Hornets' owner George Shinn after the announcement that Larry signed a 12-year contract worth an incredible $84 million.

Injuries to both Johnson and Mourning hurt the Hornets in
1993–1994. Here both stars follow the action in street clothes.
The worst thing for a great athlete is not being able to play.

Because of the back problem, Larry had to take it slow at the start of the season. He was just starting to get into shape when he suffered another injury. This one was a lower-back strain that would cause him to miss 31 games, nearly half the season. On top of that, center Alonzo Mourning had to miss 21 games because of a leg injury. With their two stars out, the Hornets struggled.

Both players returned, and the team finished strong. But their 41–41 record wasn't quite good enough for the team to make the playoffs. In 51 games, Larry averaged 16.4 points and 8.8 rebounds. His numbers were down because of the injuries. But people around the league still looked at him as a major force. When NBA all-star forward Horace Grant was asked which player gave him his toughest challenge, he answered quickly, "A healthy Larry Johnson. L.J. is strong, quick, and can hit from the outside. People don't realize it," Grant continued, "but he's a great defensive player too. He's got the whole package."

Larry Johnson has certainly come a long way from the mean streets of South Dallas. Yet when he returns to that city he often drives back to his old neighborhood.

Larry regularly goes head-to-head with the greatest power forwards in the league. One of them, Chicago's Horace Grant (in glasses), called Larry his toughest challenge.

Larry's rough childhood in South Dallas has given him a soft spot for children. Here he signs autographs for kids at the basketball camp he has run each summer at the YMCA in Morehead, North Carolina.

"I park near the [Green Bay Park] court, pop the trunk, and play music from the speakers," he said. "Everybody comes around and we talk. There could be the greatest party ever just across the street and I wouldn't go. I'd rather just stand there and talk with the people."

One time a policeman came by. He saw the late-model, high-priced car and the crowd. When he ran a check on the plates he learned the car belonged to Larry Johnson. The policeman then pulled Larry aside and warned him that this was a place of trouble, and he expressed his surprise that Larry would want to be there.

Larry stood up and pointed to a window just across the street from the court.

"See that," he said. "That's where I lived. This is where I spent most of my life. Why shouldn't I be here? This is home. I don't forget home."

LARRY JOHNSON: HIGHLIGHTS

1969	Born on March 14 in Tyler, Texas.
1987	Named U.S. High School Player of the Year in his senior year at Skyline High School in Dallas, Texas. Enters Odessa (Texas) Junior College.
1988	Selected College Freshman Player of the Year. Chosen Junior College Player of the Year.
1989	Again named Junior College Player of the Year. Named All-American. Enters University of Nevada at Las Vegas (UNLV) as a junior.
1990	First UNLV player to be named consensus All-American. UNLV wins NCAA (National Collegiate Athletic Association) national championship.
1991	Named consensus All-American again. Wins James Naismith Award and John Wooden Award, both given to the athlete considered best college player of the year. Drafted by and subsequently joins the Charlotte Hornets of the National Basketball Association (NBA).
1992	Chosen the NBA's Rookie of the Year.
1993	Selected to start in NBA All-Star Game. Leads Charlotte to its first-ever winning season and first-ever appearance in NBA Playoffs. Named to All-NBA Second Team. Signs contract worth approximately $84 million over 12 years.
1994	Misses 31 games due to back injuries, as Hornets fail to reach playoffs.

FIND OUT MORE

Duden, Jane and Susan Osberg. *Basketball*. New York: Macmillan, 1991.

Gutman, Bill. *Basketball*. North Bellmore, N.Y.: Marshall Cavendish, 1990.

Slammin', Jammin', and Dunkin'. Racine, Wisc.: Western Publishing, 1993.

Superstars and Super Stats. Racine, Wisc.: Western Publishing, 1992.

How to write to
Larry Johnson:

Larry Johnson
c/o The Charlotte Hornets
1 Hive Drive
Charlotte, NC 28217

INDEX

VOLCANOES

VOLCANOES

PETER MURRAY
THE CHILD'S WORLD®

The Klickitat Indians called it Fire Mountain, but for over 100 years it had done nothing but sleep.

People vacationing at beautiful Spirit Lake would gaze up at its majestic, snow-capped peak and think, "How quiet and peaceful it is here."

The mountain looked as though it would be there forever. But in March 1980, the mountain grumbled and the earth trembled. Plumes of steam appeared above the peak, and the face of the mountain slowly began to change shape.

Mount St. Helens had awakened, and it wasn't feeling peaceful anymore.

Sixty miles beneath our feet lies a layer of hot, half-molten rock called the *mantle*. Enormous *crustal plates,* thousands of miles across, float like rafts on this ocean of soft stone, fitting together like the pieces of a giant jigsaw puzzle. These plates push against each other or pull apart, moving so slowly that they might take a hundred years or more to travel an inch.

The seam between two crustal plates is called a *fault line.* When crustal plates pull apart or crash against each other, we can feel the earth shift beneath our feet. This movement is called an *earth tremor,* or *earthquake.*

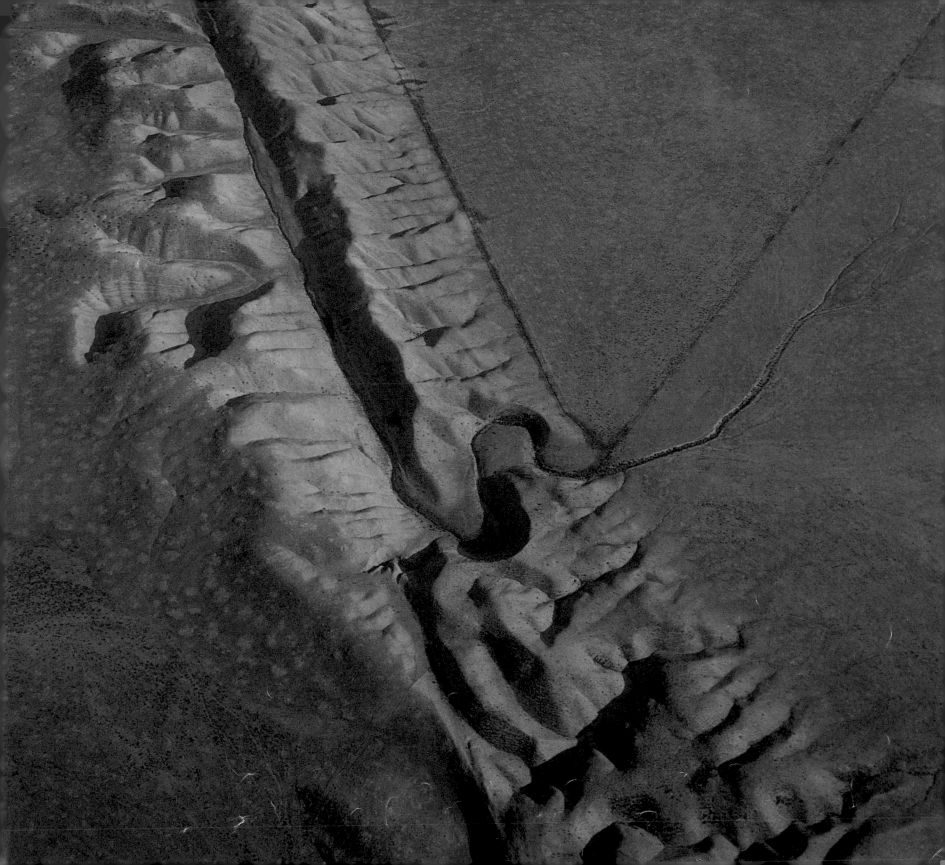

In certain parts of the world, the movement of the crustal plates causes cracks to form deep underground, all the way down to the mantle. Molten rock called *magma* fills the cracks, rising up through the crust toward the surface. A volcano forms when magma *erupts* onto the earth's surface.

Most volcanoes form at the edges of crustal plates. The volcanoes of Alaska, Japan, the Philippines, South America, and Mexico are on the edge of the Pacific Ocean Plate. This circle of active volcanoes is called the "Ring of Fire."

Mount St. Helens is one of those volcanoes.

Mount St. Helens is located in the Cascade Mountains. The Cascades are the remains of old volcanoes that have been *dormant,* or inactive, for hundreds of years. The last time Mount St. Helens had erupted was in 1857. Since then, all had been quiet in the Cascades. Until 1980.

Volcanologists—scientists who study volcanoes—heard about the earth tremors near Mount St. Helens. They were worried that the dormant volcano was getting ready to erupt again. Over the next few weeks, the rumbling grew louder. People who lived near the mountain were told to leave their homes.

Volcanoes called *shield volcanoes* form when magma flows out onto the earth's surface. These volcanoes build up slowly. Magma oozes up from below the earth's crust and flows down the sides of the volcano. This river of molten rock is so hot that it burns up anything it touches. When magma flows out onto the surface, it is called *lava*.

Hawaii's active volcanoes are shield volcanoes.

Other planets also have shield volcanoes. Olympus Mons, the tallest mountain on Mars, is an extinct shield volcano more than 50 miles high!

A *cinder cone volcano* is created when lava erupts in the form of ash and cinders. In 1943, a farmer in Mexico was working in his field when the earth shook and a crack appeared in the ground. Smoke and ash billowed skyward. Sparks and glowing rocks flew into the air, setting nearby trees on fire.

The next morning, a pile of ash and lava 35 feet high stood in the middle of his field! And it was still growing. A few days later a cone-shaped volcano almost 500 feet tall covered the surrounding fields. It was named Parîcutin. Today, Parîcutin is a volcanic mountain over 1,000 feet high.

When the edge of one plate pushes over another, magma can be forced to the surface. The biggest volcanoes on Earth, called *composite volcanoes,* often form in these areas. Composite volcanoes aren't picky. They erupt with a combination of ash, smoke, molten lava, and huge chunks of stone—sometimes as big as a house!

Mount Fuji, Japan's tallest mountain, is a dormant composite volcano. When they are active, composite volcanoes can be extremely dangerous. In the year 79 A.D., Mount Vesuvius erupted and buried the city of Pompeii, killing 16,000 people.

Mount St. Helens is a composite volcano, too.

Volcanologists feared that eventually, Mount St. Helens would erupt with deadly force. But no one expected the tremendous blast that shook the earth on May 18, 1980. After four weeks of tremors and small eruptions, Mount St. Helens exploded with a force as great as 500 atom bombs. Nine miles away, trees were flattened by the force of the blast. Forests were buried beneath six feet of ash. A gray cloud rose miles into the air, darkening the sky. Nine hours later, after the smoke cleared, Mount St. Helens was 1,000 feet shorter—the mountain had blown its top!

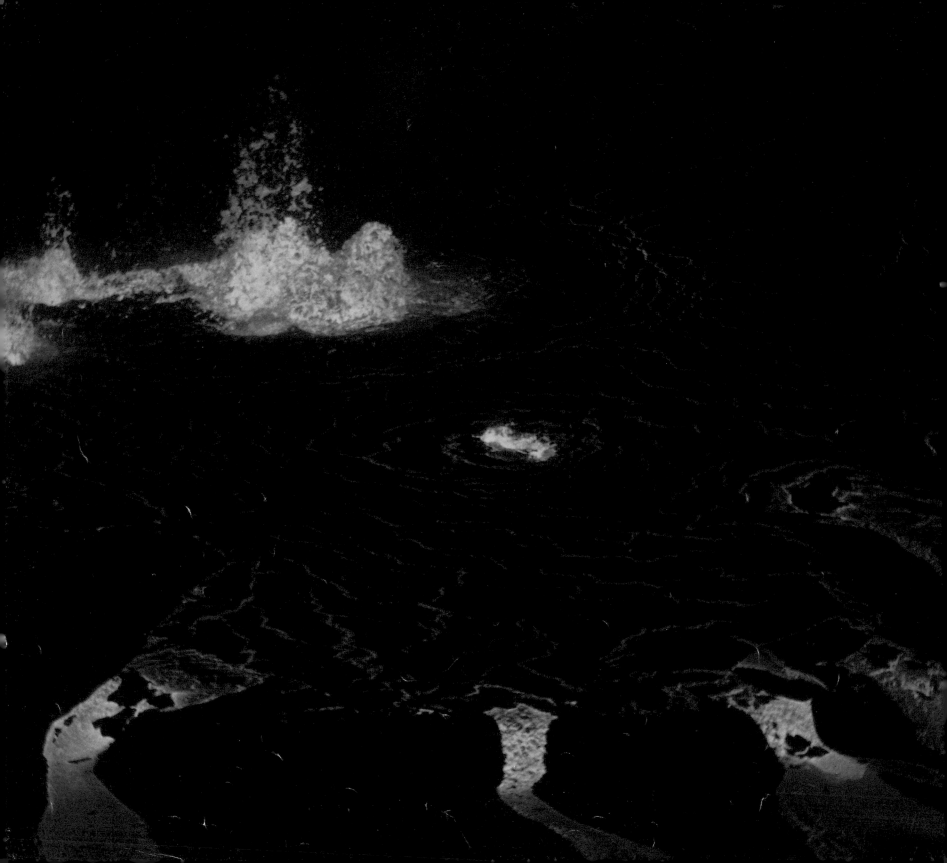

Volcanoes are found not only on Earth's continents, but also under the sea. Sometimes an undersea volcano will build up so much lava that it will form an island. The Hawaiian Islands were formed by a string of volcanoes. Some of these volcanoes are underwater, and still growing! Many years from now, a new Hawaiian island will emerge from the sea.

The loudest sound in history was caused when Krakatoa, a volcanic island in the Indian Ocean, exploded in 1883. The sound of the explosion was heard by people 2,000 miles away. The entire island of Krakatoa disappeared into the sea. Since then a new volcanic cone has appeared, and the island is rebuilding itself.

When a volcano like Mount St. Helens destroys forests and homes, we see it as a disaster. But good things come from volcanoes, too. Volcanoes have been spewing gases, lava, and ash for billions of years. Volcanic gases formed Earth's first atmosphere, long before life began on the planet. To this day, ash settles on the soil and makes crops grow more easily. And people are now using the power of volcanoes. In Iceland, where there are several active volcanoes, heat from lava beds is piped into homes to warm them in the winter. In the future, you might even be eating food cooked by volcano power!

INDEX

PHOTO RESEARCH
Kristee Flynn

PHOTO CREDITS
SCIENCE PHOTO LIBRARY/Matthew Shipp:
front cover
COMSTOCK/Georg Gerster: 2, 11, 24
COMSTOCK/Janet Wishnetsky: 14
COMSTOCK/Van Garmon: 27
COMSTOCK/Harold Kinne: 28
PHOTO RESEARCHERS/Pat & Tom Leeson: 4
PHOTO RESEARCHERS/John Meehan: 7
SCIENCE SOURCE/Krafft/Explorer: 8, 21
BRUCE COLEMAN, INC./G.D. Plage: 13
BRUCE COLEMAN, INC./W. Ferchland
Rob & Melissa Simpson: 17
EARTHVIEWS/James D. Watt: 18
USGS/WEATHERSTOCK: 31

Library of Congress Cataloging-in-Publication Data
Murray, Peter, 1952 Sept. 29-
Volcanoes / by Peter Murray.
p. cm.
Includes Index.
ISBN 1-56766-197-1
1. Volcanoes--Juvenile literature.   [1. Volcanoes.]   I. Title.
QE521.3.M87 5   1995   95-3515
551.2′1--dc20